I0106391

What Was It Like Fooding in the 80s?

A Journal to Revisit and Share 80s Totally Tubular Eats

~ Riya Aarini ~

What Was It Like Fooding in the 80s?
A Journal to Revisit and Share 80s Totally Tubular Eats
Text Copyright © 2025 by Riya Aarini

All rights reserved.
First printed in the United States of America.
The author supports copyright. Thank you for purchasing an authorized edition of this book and for complying with copyright laws by not distributing, scanning, or copying this book in any form without express permission.
Images licensed from Shutterstock.

ISBN: 978-1-956496-74-1 (paperback)
ISBN: 978-1-956496-75-8 (hardcover)

www.riyapresents.com

This book belongs to '80s foodie

_____

_____

Contents

BON APPETIT

Welcome to Your '80s Food History!

The decade of excess proved to be no less extravagant in its food aspirations. The 1980s saw the bold introduction of culinary delights, from the imposing seven-layer dip to the resourceful potato skins, that rocked the vibrant party scenes.

Buffet restaurants drew countless hungry patrons, many of whom skipped a meal or two in order to get the most bang for their buck—eating all they could for one attractive price. Nothing expressed indulgence more than '80s all-you-can-eat buffets!

The gastronomic fun didn't stop there. Ethnic foods, like sushi and Tex-Mex, catapulted to stardom in the '80s, satisfying the tastes of adventurers seeking exotic flavors. Health foods started taking off with a flurry of low-fat options too.

Whether you're a food connoisseur or a true '80s foodie who believes the era's mouthwatering cuisines offered unique appeal, this prompt journal will stir up those special food memories. Here's to the smorgasbord of totally tubular '80s food!

Cheese Fondue

Cheese fondue grew to be an '80s food phenomenon, inspiring entire
restaurants to open.

**Did your family own a fondue pot? If so, on what occasions
did you use it?**

**If you fondued, what foods did you dip into the melting cheese
pot? Bread, fruit?**

Did your family hold fondue nights?

What scintillating taste memories did '80s fondue create?

Parties

Describe the impressiveness of seven-layer dip, with its base of refried beans and layers of sour cream, zesty salsa, guacamole, tangy olives, and loads of cheese.

Did your '80s parties include shrimp cocktails? Were they a hit?

How gnarly were potato skins? This popular '80s party food stole the show, with hollowed-out skins topped with crispy bacon and oodles of cheese.

Did the '80s bread bowl and cheesy dip trend take off in your household?

Pizza rolls pleased '80s crowds. Did you relish these savory bites?

Recount whether you salivated for sloppy joe nachos in the '80s.

Did you join the '80s deviled eggs craze?

What popular '80s desserts did you eat at parties? Luxurious
Viennetta ice cream, Baked Alaska?

Ethnic Foods

Ethnic cuisine was less common in the '80s. However, exotic dishes started finding their way onto dining tables due to growing interest in diverse and venturesome menu options, as well as increasing immigration.

How far did you travel for ethnic food in the '80s?

Were you familiar with Thai, Indian, or Brazilian food in the '80s?

Japanese

Did you eat sushi in the '80s? If so, where did you get it from?

How "hip" was eating sushi during the era?

Chinese

How often did you eat Chinese food?

What Chinese foods did you enjoy? Sweet-and-sour pork, fried rice, chow mein?

Mexican

How were you introduced to Mexican food in the '80s?

Did you have a taste for Tex-Mex, a fusion of Mexican and American cuisine?

Summer BBQs

What did you barbecue during '80s summers? Burgers, ribeye steaks, chicken?

Name the sides that accompanied the grilled food. Coleslaw, potato salad, corn on the cob?

Did you grill pineapples in the '80s? If so, describe the burst of sweet, smoky flavors.

What beverages washed down your BBQ fare?

Was summer barbecuing a family tradition?

Describe the scents from '80s summer BBQs. Smoke wafting from the grill, chlorine from the pool, cigarettes...

20

Ice Cream

When the ice cream truck pulled up, what did you order?

How amazing were strawberry shortcake ice cream bars in the '80s?

Did you hang out at ice cream shops in the '80s? If so, name your favorite shop.

How enticing were '80s ice cream prices? At ten cents for a double scoop, did you have nickels left over to buy something else?

What cool memories did '80s ice cream create?

Cookies

Mini, everyday indulgences, '80s cookies were beloved by millions.

Name one cookie you found irresistible in the '80s.

How did you like your chocolate chip cookies? Soft, crunchy, a bit of both?

Describe the most unique cookie you tried in the '80s.

Did you ever try to recreate a recipe from your favorite cookie store? If so, how did you obtain the recipe, and did it meet your expectations?

What was the most iconic cookie you'd bitten into in the '80s?

What ingredients gave it the wow factor?

Was it homemade? If so, who baked it?

If it was store-bought, from where did you buy it? Recount whether a line of customers wrapped around the store.

Holidays

Mardi Gras

Mardi Gras dishes included jambalaya, muffuletta sandwiches, shrimp creole, and crawfish boil. People also feasted on sweet treats, like beignets, pancakes, and bananas foster.

What savory foods did you enjoy during Mardis Gras in the '80s?

What sweet treats did you eat on Fat Tuesday in the '80s?

Did you or your family fry paczkis? Or did you purchase the fried doughnuts from a bakery?

What type of paczki filling did you prefer? Jam, cream, fruit?

Did you ever receive a colorful slice of king cake with the baby figurine hidden inside? If so, describe your reaction.

If you found the figurine inside, did you host the next king cake party?

St. Patrick's Day

On St. Patrick's Day, did you wake up to an Irish breakfast?

If so, did the hearty morning meal satisfy you over the whole day?

How much corned beef, cabbage, and potatoes did you consume on St. Patrick's Day in the '80s?

What dessert finished off your St. Patrick's Day meal? Minty green grasshopper pie, something else?

Memorial Day

Did you picnic on Memorial Day with family or friends? What foods and drinks did you set out on the picnic table or blanket?

Did you hold cookouts to welcome the unofficial start of summer?

How many hot dogs did you consume during hot dog season (Memorial Day through Labor Day)?

How creative did you get with hot dog toppings? Relish, sauerkraut, pickles?

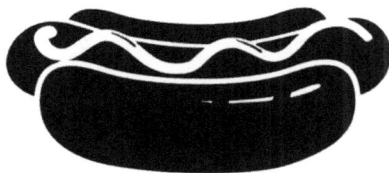

Thanksgiving

Name the main course of your '80s Thanksgiving dinners.

If turkey took center stage, describe how it was prepared. Roasted, stuffed, glazed?

Did you use Thanksgiving recipes passed down through the generations? If so, name one recipe.

What side dishes did your family include with Thanksgiving meals? Common sides included green bean casserole, mashed potatoes, and rolls.

Sweet potato casserole, rich with gooey marshmallows and crunchy pecans, as well as classic pumpkin pie with a giant dollop of whipped cream, were '80s Thanksgiving dessert favorites.

Describe the desserts you enjoyed during '80s Thanksgiving meals.

Recount a Thanksgiving Day fiasco, such as burning the bird to a crisp or carving accidents.

Did the disaster turn out well in the end? If not, how did you recover from it?

Do you look back on this Thanksgiving fail with humor?

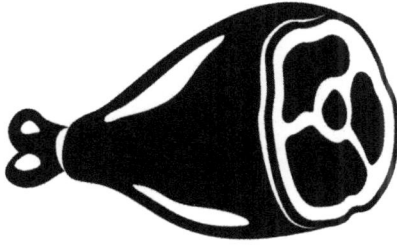

Christmas

Christmas meals in the '80s included baked ham topped with pineapple slices, mini meat pies, and cheese balls. Dessert might've been upside-down fruitcake, sweet-and-tart ribbon gelatin, or a chocolate yule log.

What savory foods did you devour on Christmas in the '80s?

What desserts did you crave during Christmas in the '80s?

How did you navigate receiving fruitcake?

Describe an '80s kitchen disaster that made cooking on Christmas a day to remember. Heavy snowfall causing power outages, the dog devouring the turkey?

How many people did this event impact?

Does your family retell this tale, laughing until they cry?

New Year's Day

What foods started New Year's Day in the '80s?

Name a drink with which you toasted friends and family on
New Year's Day.

Restaurants

Bennigan's, serving robust Irish fare, Polynesian-themed Trader Vic's, Chi-Chi's with its Tex-Mex enchiladas, and kid-friendly Bullwinkle's were popular '80s restaurant chains.

Did you eat at restaurants on special occasions or regularly? If on special occasions, which ones?

Did you ever dine at a restaurant with a star–studded clientele, like politicians and movie stars? If so, which restaurant?

What was your favorite '80s restaurant?

What did you appreciate most about the restaurant? Scrumptious food, impeccable service, ambiance?

If it's no longer open, does it inspire a sense of food nostalgia?

Fast Food

Did you regularly or rarely eat fast food in the '80s?

Were visits to fast-food restaurants big events?

Looking back, what do you think of '80s fast-food prices?

What '80s fast food do you still crave today?

Buffet Restaurants

Buffet restaurants in the '80s drew crowds. People ate heartily at chains, like Ponderosa Steakhouse, Bonanza, and Old Country Buffet. All-you-can-eat buffet restaurants offered a diverse assortment of dishes, satisfying even the pickiest family members. Reasonable prices doubled their appeal.

What was the allure of '80s buffet restaurants? Affordable prices, no wait times, a welcome opportunity to overeat?

Did you skip a meal prior to visiting the buffet restaurant?

How much wasted food did you see at buffet restaurants?

Do you wish buffet restaurants would return with '80s fervor? Why or why not?

Leftovers

What did your family do with leftovers in the '80s? Create brand-new meals?

If so, what new dishes did leftovers inspire? Shepherd's pie, meatloaf, pasta salad?

What types of containers did you use to store leftovers?

Portion Sizes

Portion sizes ballooned in the '80s, leading to even restaurants serving up more food. Everyday fare, like bags of chips, are now half the size they were in the glorious decade of excess.

How would you describe '80s portion sizes?

Did you consume more food in the '80s as a result?

Sandwiches

Sandwiches were household staples in the '80s, ranging from popular grilled cheese to BLTs and the never-fail-to-satisfy peanut butter and jelly.

Name your favorite sandwich fillings from the '80s. Cheese slices, meat cuts, egg salad?

Did you add generous amounts of mayonnaise or butter to enhance the richness of sandwiches?

How did you like your grilled cheese in the '80s?

Did you dunk your sandwiches? If so, in what?

How inventive did you get with sandwiches in the '80s? Crushed potato chips inside?

Do you still prepare these sandwiches for a taste of nostalgia?

Gardens

Did your family grow food in a garden? If so, what did you harvest?

Which garden veggies made it to your dinner plate?

Did you can homegrown foods in the '80s? If so, which ones?

How many canned foods did you store in the cellar or kitchen cupboards?

Potlucks

Common '80s potluck dishes included Swedish meatballs, chicken pot pie, and taco salad.

Did you host or attend potlucks in the '80s? If you attended, what did you bring?

If you hosted, what foods did guests bring?

Birthdays

Did you enjoy special meals on your birthdays? If so, what did they consist of?

Did loved ones treat you to cookie cakes on your birthdays in the '80s?

Did you prefer the giant frosted cookies rather than traditional cakes on your birthdays?

Name your favorite birthday cookie cake variation. Chocolate chip, oatmeal raisin, peanut butter?

Food Flashes
from the '80s Past

Food Flashes
from the '80s Past

Breakfasts

What was your go-to breakfast food in the '80s?

Did you eat sugary cereals? If so, name your favorite(s).

Which cartoons influenced your cereal choices?

Did your family buy cereals for the collectible or toy inside the box?

Did you buy cereal boxes to collect the proofs of purchase required to obtain free prizes?

If so, name a fun prize you received.

Did you visit fast food restaurants for breakfast? If so, which ones? What did you typically order?

Which '80s convenience foods satisfied your morning taste buds? Toaster pastries, pizza bagels, breakfast burritos?

How nutritiously did you eat for breakfast in the '80s? Oatmeal, yogurt, fruit?

List the foods prepared for Sunday morning brunches. Eggs, biscuits, sausages?

Lunches

If you ate Lunchables, did customizing the mini sandwiches turn lunch into a fun event?

Did you eat a lot of processed or prepackaged foods at lunch? If so, provide an example.

85

How many peanut butter and jelly sandwiches did you consume in the '80s?

What hearty lunches did you eat in the '80s?

How much ingenuity went into making casserole and lasagna lunches in your household?

Dinners

Spaghetti, stew, and chicken were common '80s dinner courses.

List three typical dinners you ate in the '80s.

_____

_____

_____

Name an epic '80s dinner menu item. What did you enjoy most about it?

Did you consume mostly homemade dinners during the era?

How often did you microwave dinners? Was it primarily to heat leftovers?

Were frozen foods or TV dinners a regular part of your evening meals?

Did you eat a lot of canned foods? Canned soups, canned vegetables?

Describe one memorable '80s dinner and why it stands out.
Melding of flavors, good company, something else?

Snacks

Name three tubular '80s snacks you munched on.

_____

_____

_____

Where did you consume these snacks? Maxin' and relaxin' next to the pool, on the porch?

Do you wish the beloved '80s pudding pops would make a comeback?

Which '80s snacks bring back good memories?

Fruits

Name the summer fruits you noshed on in the '80s.

How often did you eat fresh fruit?

Did you nibble on Sunkist Fun Fruits or Fruit Wrinkles in the '80s? If so, do you miss these popular fruit snacks?

Chocolate

Chocolate bars, from PB Max to Bar None, offered moments of sheer rapture.

Did you eat chocolate in the '80s? If so, how often?

Name three irresistible chocolate bars.

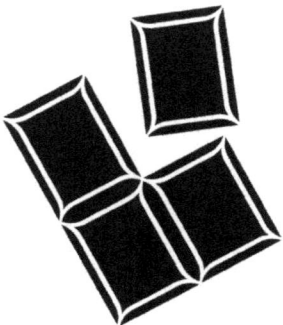

_____

_____

_____

Where did you buy chocolate bars in the '80s? Grocery stores, vending machines?

Do today's chocolate bars taste the same as the original '80s versions?

What discontinued '80s chocolate bars do you wish made a comeback?

Candy

A wide range of candy, like Nerds, Pop Rocks, and Jolly Ranchers, offered awesome taste sensations.

Which candies did you favor most during the era?

Did you eat candy cigarettes in the '80s?

If so, what do you think about the name change to "candy sticks"?

Are candy sticks nostalgic treats for you today?

Bakeries

How often did you visit bakeries in the '80s?

Name the bakery you frequented most often.

Popular '80s bakery items included upside-down pineapple cakes, snickerdoodles, and ice cream cakes.

What baked goods did you treat yourself to?

Describe the aromas wafting out of your favorite '80s bakery.

If you catch a whiff of these scents today, what do they remind you of? Celebrations, home, something else?

Grocery Stores

Did you ever fill up on grocery store samples?

If so, name an appetizing sample you returned to for seconds, thirds...

Did your local grocery store carry global spices and ingredients?

How much variety did you see in '80s grocery produce sections?

Beverages

Juices

Popular juices included Capri-Sun, Hi-C Ecto Cooler, and Hawaiian Punch in a can.

What fruity beverages did you drink in the '80s?

Did you prefer the canned or boxed versions?

How did the container affect the taste, if at all?

Name one mondo cool juice flavor.

Milkshakes

Where did you buy milkshakes? In the school cafeteria, restaurants?

Were milkshake machines stationed throughout your school in the '80s?

If so, how heavenly was it to pump out milkshakes?

Which milkshake flavor hit the spot?

Sodas

Soda consumption soared in the '80s and included vintage colas, like Jolt, Tab, and Life Savers Soda.

Which fizzy soda did you enjoy most in the '80s?

At what hours did you drink soda? Mornings, afternoons, evenings?

Which discontinued '80s soda do you wish you could sip again?

Homecooked Foods

Who primarily cooked meals in your home in the '80s?

What dishes did they prepare? Lasagna, tacos, casseroles?

How much did you help with the preparations?

Do you make any of these homecooked foods today?

Comfort Foods

Hearty and filling, comfort foods in the '80s were meant to be savored. They included tater tot casseroles, sloppy joes, and meatloaf, among a wide range of other satisfying dishes.

Name three comfort foods that gave you a feeling of well-being in the '80s.

_____

_____

_____

Did loved ones feed you these dishes when you felt sad or got sick with the cold or flu?

What gave these foods that comforting quality?

Did you add any twists to macaroni and cheese, a popular '80s comfort food? If so, what?

Does the mere aroma of '80s comfort foods bring back good memories?

Recipes

Describe Mom's most timeless recipe.

If Dad cooked, name one of his totally bodacious recipes.

Which of Grandma's recipes could no one prepare better?

Did your local organizations sell spiralbound cookbooks as fundraisers? Did you buy any and prepare the recipes?

Did you inherit recipes from relatives? If so, name one that you still use today.

Did you ever come up with original recipes? If so, describe one and the '80s ingredients you used to prepare it.

What dish was your state best known for? Maryland crab cakes, Maine lobster rolls...

How often did you prepare this dish at home?

Did you use a family recipe to create it?

What was your town's most iconic dish? Chicago deep-dish pizza, San Diego fish tacos...

Did you enjoy this dish homecooked or at restaurants?

If at home, how did you obtain the recipe?

Name the wackiest recipe you tried. How did it turn out? Was it a crowd-pleaser?

Healthy Eating

How concerned were you about eating nutritiously in the '80s?

Did you opt for low-fat foods, like cheese or sour cream?

Did TV public service announcements (PSAs) influence your food choices?

Do you believe '80s foods contained more preservatives, dyes, and artificial flavors?

How often did salads accompany your '80s meals?

How many salad dressing options were available in the '80s?

Did you opt for homemade dressing?

Had you heard about quinoa in the '80s?

How confused were you about the '80s flip-flopping PSAs that warned eggs were unhealthy, then healthy...

Food Intangibles

How many daily meals did you eat in the '80s? Did you graze or snack in between?

Did '80s TV commercials inspire your food choices? If so, recount one influential commercial.

Did convenience dictate the type of meals you ate in the
'80s?

Describe the longest time you waited in line to buy a food item in the '80s. What was the food, and was it worth the wait?

Did meals inspire feelings of togetherness?

How important were sit-down family meals to you in the '80s?

What discontinued '80s foods do you miss most?

Which '80s food held special meaning for you, and why?

Did food simply taste better in the '80s?

Sum up '80s food in one word.

_____

More Food Flashes from the '80s Past

More Food Flashes from the '80s Past

Long Live '80s Eats!

No matter what the era, food will always hold a special place in people's hearts. Meals are the focal points of not only everyday life but celebrations and milestones.

Answering these prompts might've returned you to the best of '80s foods and the important events surrounding them. Sharing the completed journal gives friends and family insights into a sweet slice of the irreplicable '80s food culture you are privileged to have been a part of.

That's awesome sauce!

Books in the
What Was It Like series

What Was It Like Growing Up in the 70s?
A Journal to Revisit and Share the Groovy 70s

What Was It Like Growing Up in the 80s?
A Journal to Revisit and Share the Totally Awesome 80s

What Was It Like During Christmas in the 80s?
A Journal to Revisit and Share the 80s Holiday Spirit

What Was It Like Growing Up in the 90s?
A Journal to Revisit and Share the Rad 90s

What Was It Like During Christmas in the 90s?
A Journal to Revisit and Share the 90s Holiday Vibe

What Was It Like Marrying in the 90s?
A Journal (for Her) to Revisit and Share 90s Wedding
Magic

www.riyapresents.com

www.ingramcontent.com/pod-product-compliance
Lightning Source LLC
Chambersburg PA
CBHW052020030426
42335CB00026B/3227

* 9 7 8 1 9 5 6 4 9 6 7 4 1 *